I0190210

In
sanity

by
Bradley Smith

In
sanity

by Bradley Smith

Southern
Arizona
Press

Southern Arizona Press
Sierra Vista, Arizona

In sanity

By Bradley Smith

First Edition

Content Copyright © 2024 by Bradley Smith

All rights reserved.

Except as permitted under the Copyright Act of 1976, no portion of this book may be reproduced or distributed in any form, or by any means, or stored in a database or retrieval system, without prior written permission of the author or the publisher.

Author: Bradley Smith
Editor: Paul Gilliland
Formatting: Southern Arizona Press

Interior Artwork: Hugo Machado
Used with permission of artist

Front Cover Artwork: Devon from Create Vista
Back Cover Artwork: serezniy from Create Vista
Royalty free images used under Pro Subscription Plan

Published by Southern Arizona Press
Sierra Vista, Arizona 85635
www.SouthernArizonaPress.com

ISBN: 978-1-960038-52-4

Poetry

The psychotic drowns in the same waters in which the mystic swims with delight."
— Joseph Campbell

Introduction

The sirens are back, calling me towards the shore once more. I thought I was happy at sea, but I was drowning in the wild waters. Where the mystics swim with delight, I was choking on pills and alcohol.

So here I am again. Contained by my split mind. Confronted now with the unpleasant idea. Am I once again insane, and have I tumbled too far? Or like last time, is recovery possible?

My mind was split once more, though I thought I was clear. Then the ambulance showed, and I was gripped with insanity. A vicious cycle of medication and mental wards, this is what this book discuses. I was falling, like so many before me, and I didn't even know how deep that insanity hole went, but it went deep ... In this collection I will continue to be honest with you, about all the nonsense schizophrenia can bring. I still sing along to songs badly, and I still struggle with my mental health. In this poetry book I will go deeper, into my long stay at the mental ward and one massive step back in my sanity. So here you are if you want to peek into an unstable mind, and the recovery that takes place through my therapy, which happens to be poetry. In my last book my mind split, and this time it cracked again. This is me healing, and hopefully it heals some part of you as well. That is the goal. So welcome to my collection, I hope you enjoy

Contents

Light   66

Darkness

In sanity

Have I lost my mind?
I say to my reflection
Injections are soon to come
I think my sanity is done
I will find you through infinite space
As insanity takes my special place
Such a strange face that I've been gifted

In sane.
It's night, and I look for a light
But it's broken like my brain
Oh, the strain. Oh, it's strange
I see demons and angels
I see illusions and delusions
At the time I thought I was alright
Welcome to my night
Where the birds no longer sing
And I am one crazy thing
An animal controlled by the subliminal
Where the message is only

In
Sanity

Next Episode

I feel the darkness enter
Muttering again to myself
The lights seem brighter than usual
All these thoughts are fluttering
Am I losing my mind again?

I try to gain some semblance
Then the ambulance shows its horns
A siren calling me to my next home for awhile
Luring me in, the voices are yelling
Come closer to us!

Multiple shadows and formless thoughts
Barking back and forth like wild dogs
Off the leash as sanity seems reach less
I'm speechless that I am here.
A split mind once more

Psychosis

My mind is cracked
It's leaking onto the streets
All the clouds are closing in
A storm is brewing inside

These delusions are becoming my reality
Walking off the track of the guided path
Diving in the deep end, and I'm drowning
I can't swim there anymore

Am I talking to myself?
Is that so crazy?

I feel the padded walls approaching
I feel the hospital doors closing
My mind is taking in too much noise
Whispers are coming from angels and devils. This is
psychosis

Will I see sanity ever again?

Hospitalized

The doors close
The electronic button buzzes
My mind is fragmented and loose
One shot to muzzle me

I find my bed quickly and lay down
I was way too crazy to be running around town.
The nurse smiles and I frown
I listen for the voices, but they don't make a sound.
I'm a caged bird,
I'm a sleeper who refuses to dream
While I was out running wild.
I only found imaginary friends on my team.
Now, here I am in this mental ward
It's going to be a long stay this time
Feeling down like a junkie who never scored.
As the needles replace my happy rhymes.
I ask the nurse if I can go
She looks me straight in the eyes and sadly replies.

No

Grand Rising

Another grand rising, but I don't feel so grand today.
I pace and pace, it's still so hard to believe I am back
in this place
My knees crack like thunder, from all the trauma I've
been under
But the sun rises once more, and as it rises I do as
well.
Soon I know I'll be out that door, with one little story
to tell.

Decaffeinated

No caffeine for this mental fiend
Inside the ward it's a war on awake
Sleep it takes hold in here, so I sip anyway
My friends-tired eyes as his body sways

Another day it begins

I sit outside and watch the birds
As the birds inside watch me
Nurses are nursing decaf as well
The paper cup swirls. This black pool

The sun is rising
I fall into the plush seats outside
My friend has angels that he confides in
But I don't see them. Perhaps too much sin
The reason he speaks to the glass slide

I am falling
The percentage is weak, like my will,
Still, it offers a slight comforting hug
No mug, just a double cup of darkness
If only I had one cigarette to spark

And I dream...

Typical
(dedicated to anti-psychotic medication)

Injection point
No ointment
Can heal these wounds
Wound and bound arms
And the needle goes in.

Rejecting authorities
Has its calamities
As the poison enters
Blocking my receptors
Please...
Another timeless morn
My skin splits and is torn
To the point of no return
The dopamine drains
A sharp refrain...
Laying back in my death rows chair
The pinch I take, though still fear
My toes curl, welcome to a junkie's world
Where we dive headfirst into the void
And I succumb,

Typical...

The Pen

If I could fly
Above these institutions
I wonder what I would do?
Would I swoop down to see you?
Or stay in the stars?

If I did sink
Stuck down with you
I wonder how my split mind would think?
Would I just sleep to see my dreams?
No form of freedom now it seems

If I did just stay here forever
Locked in this place
Would I be one good dog and lay?
Beg for my feed and for forgiveness
Or stay high and look at those who have less.
Questions always on my mind
Sitting here in this pen
So, this is for you my caged friend
It turns out. I can't fly in the end.

Delusion

The confusion of my sizzling mind
This is your brain on drugs they say
Full moon and sleepless nights, teeth on the grind
Pockets empty, so it's my soul I must pay
Clouds closing closely on my back
My foggy brain full of strange ideas
Hospital doors are open seems the only facts
With tired blood shot eyes full of tears
I see them dressed in white coats
They strap me in, ready for the crazy ride
Floating through delusion, arrives a chemical lifeboat
This ocean of sanity floods in like the tide
Where am I? Locked in hell, I think.
Then an angel enters silently
Takes my mana, and leaves abruptly
My eyes close and the night expires
The bright light shines through shades and wakes me.
A strange clarity is felt.
I'm locked away but oddly free
I look up. Free and clear
And it is your smiling face that I see…

Ashamed

Recovery is now entrenched in my blood.
As sanity seeps through my pores
Insanity came through like a flood
I messed with people, messed with stores

An ancient Egyptian god once spoke to me
Tales of the red sea and how it did part
My lines were penned unconsciously
To you it may be nonsense. To me it was art

An ancient scroll on papyrus predicted my fate.
At least that's where my mind's eye travelled
I was so full of confusions weight
A hospital bed held down is what unraveled

Lessons now have been shown in dreams
Of how crazy my mind can wonder when not tamed
As the straps release or so it seems
As I was bound, and completely ashamed.

Lonely Boy

A couple missed on Christmas
One message from them
A couple calls from him
Still, I sank that cask

It was one lonely new year
Just myself and whiskey
It seems somethings stay the same
But listen, the bottle never lasts

As for easter, I'm in the ward again
This mental warfare always creeps in
I need a resurrection just like him
Really though, I crave a bottle of gin

What will happen next, is up to God
And the spirits I guess, yes,
That I wish I didn't rely, but,
I try and ask why, and still

No reply...

Clear

I feel like an outcast of society
Un kept and out of touch
Withering away in my own sadness
Glooming over my madness
Another pathetic poem!
I always lack hope when needed
I'd much rather be drunk and weeded
But I am broke!
Broken down and financially poor
This voice inside still yells, more, more.
One more toke please!
For days and days, I would hide away
Smoking away my life. I was fading
Though in a moment of reflection
I Looked for hope.
But I am hopeless!
But wait, what if this time I try to heal?
If I pour out everything that I do feel?
Perhaps I can change as these chemicals rearrange
A little glimpse of hope. I'm off the dope now

A clear head I've found.

Alcohol

Addiction
Lucifer
Crucifixion
Oppression
Holes
Odious
Loneliness

Two Sides
(For those with Bipolar)

Every coin has two sides
But they both still cost the same
Trust me though, you are not to blame
Icy sometimes, then you feel lit like a flame

But please be glad you aren't plain
You see, us. We don't ride in their normal lanes.
The tides do flow, and I know,
living on a different plane
only increases the tears that yell

Stuck under a chemical spell
Are you up in heaven?
Or in the depths of hell?

This is the duality
But like it or not, this is your reality
Be thankful you remain an odyssey

I know it's hard but trust me
Where today, you are up, or down
There a still many sunny days to see.
I promise.

Untitled

And when the stars came crashing down,
and the darkness consumed me
I still had hope for the future
And faith the light would come back once more.

I'm out of those hospital doors now
One small step, for a split minded man
Again, it's black outside, but now I know
The light is not far off
Now I know
I'm home

Diary

As you can probably tell, my time inside the hospital was a rough one. I was out of my mind and the delusions were running rampant. It was through poetry that I found peace. A mental hospital it seems is great place for inspiration

My mind was too wild to be in the outside world, though I didn't know it at the time, I was too busy looking for aliens!

And while rough at the time, I'm glad the ambulance came and got me that day, otherwise who knows what might have happened. Here is some more poetry of the time I was finally released

The Needle

You pierce my flesh
I cannot sleep
Dripping from your eye
You cry just before you enter
I cry once you do
Oh, my dear friend
I will never miss you

Lithium
(dedicated to Kurt Cobain)

The numbness rides
My tired and spacey eyes
The drugs.

The numbers blur
I lay sleep curled
Its lithium

Back and forth my eyes race
To and fro they go
The drugs

A bullet to the brain
Right now, doesn't sound insane
Its lithium

I must maintain this,
I hear the devil's hiss
The drugs!

God whispers back
The lithium!
And I succumb...

A Clearing

Do I finally see, a clearing in this wild growth?
I made a sober oath in the wilderness; can I keep it?
Can I find my soul again,
without relying on the spirits?
These are the sober minded questions that scare me

This forest that I walked through daily
Was filled with poison ivy mainly
My skin become inflamed, just like I did within
All I had was my demons and gin

They blinded me clearly
But is this a clearing I see?

The Aftermath

The aftermath of destruction
Taught the foolish man how to function
Though he thought he was a prophet at the time.
Living off wild honey and screaming in rhyme.

A delusion of biblical proportion
Where his walk through the desert was his minds
    distortion.

Talks of angels around the good shepherd
As drunk as Noah after the flood
With that, he paid in two vials of blood
And soon went on his way

They found nothing that the clinic could cure.
Eventually they locked him away, somewhere secure

Pure madness was his only friend.

With God on his side, he continued to pray
Hour by hour, and day by day
Soon he would be released back into the wild

With one jab he was let go as he smiled.

No more delusion
No more fasting
No more God
These were his instructions

He quickly found a house to call his home
No more time to roam.
No more ravenous lips filled with wild honey and
    foam

He was a madman confused as a prophet
A composite of every ancient story
When all he was trying to find
Was God and his glory.

Reality

As the early morning sun
Rises and the day has begun
All the delusions that did not bring
In reality, turned out to be nothing but minds lies and
    all
And when my first cup became full,
In darkness I felt insanity's pull
Though now the light shined on my shadows.
Truth is, I was drowning far from the shallows
Blue with depression, and in so deep that I couldn't
    swim.
Where the mystics played, and dived on a whim, I
    drowned
So here is the reality.
Today I will watch the sun rise
With the hope today the rays, will take away the lies
So, this is reality now
No more insanity now
Today some hope of sanity
This is my new dawn

Reality...

Last Shot

One last shot
Now it's back to pills
Sanity is pulling me
I feel so hot

The stars look down on me
No more injections, I understand
A new life is the plan
I feel uncaught

Catch and release me from this plague
Insanity and other ailments I have contained.
My mental mind frame insane
Was a past life that needed to be untaught?

Now I have a future to hold
I begin again to feel cold
What of this life now I wonder?
And all these past feelings that I have fought?

One last shot.

Comfortable Feelings

Comfortable feelings
Are not where these lines are born
They come from pure darkness
When this soul of mine was torn
The pressure it bleeds onto the page
The older you get. The more trauma is caged.
Conformity, was not the life I chose
But to those happy on the farm
Producing the milk. I applaud you
The closer I get to you mother,
the more beauty I find.
Complex ideas excite me
Never swimming in the mainstream
It seems these schools are full and I don't belong.
I may be crazy but simple solutions seem not as
    strong
Competition is a young man's sport
Kind of like the idea of courting someone new.
A few have come and went like the seasons
Conclusions should never occur
What do we know when we can't see
Comfortable feelings it seems, are just not for me.

Risen

Another sun has risen
And those dreams forgiven
Past miss takes were illuminated
And in sleep they were illustrated

Shown pictures of pleasures and pain
Painted on my mind it all seemed so plain
At the moment when hope had left me
The sun is rising, and I finally see

It was not a dream, but a nightmare
You screaming I was never there
And maybe you were right,
another sun has risen

And I find the light in my eyes now
Yes, it was a dream but some how
The darkness still sticks like glue
When every night,
I think of you

Paranoid

I peel back the curtains
Looking through my dusty window
A beating heart is what my body contains
Pleasure and peace my only widow
Sorrowing mind and pounding chest
No one is close, though still no rest
Looking worried out at this strange world
Paranoid, terrified, if only I could rearrange

What more can I take?
This feeling grows too real
Thoughts of them closing in seems not fake
So, they give me these little pills to take.
Pacing back and forth in this place called home.
I hear the ever ringing, but won't answer the phone.
What I feel is the haunting hinges of my heart
The sun has just risen, I am in prison, and it's only the
    start
A paranoid void I drown in slow
Just so you know
How I feel
For me. This is real...

Aquarius Moon

A humanitarian at heart
Even though I fell on the moon
A secrete sacred hidden part
Maybe I showed to much to soon?

How to live pure in a world so cold?
Aquarius moon it watches on
Another chapter with something told
Left behind for when I'm gone

One more emotion contained in a word
This is the age my moon feels at home
My thoughts, like my mind may seem absurd
As each thought frantically roams

The moon is full and blue, just like your eyes
Controlling the waters. Controlling the tides
Us two together with no time for lies
This life lived in darkness, Aquarius moon I confide

My Morning

Golden hue on the leaves
Morning dew, the sun conceives

Another day. Another morning

Deathly dreams of darkness gone
Like that bright yellow, I have been reborn

Hello to the week
Goodbye to the weekend

While birds fly in synchronicity
Pity us humans don't do the same

I'm standing, looking out this dirty window
Wondering how I will go about my day

This is my morning
Wake up...

Roots

I am the flower
You are the soil
I will grow in your embrace
As we erase and toil
Together

Your love is a nutrient
Giving me the ability to rise
Lies don't live in our garden
So, pardon me as I blossom
To gather

More seeds for your essence
New seedlings for your presence
Presents for your effort
Effortlessly you affect me so
Together

We gather and grow
So, these paper petals will show
The pedestal I place you on
And if I do rise, and you stay
I'll remember my roots
Forever this way...

Cracked

You are not broke
You are not poor
Thinking of these words
That those use who have more.

Instead think you are rich
Not in paper but soul
In something that you cannot hold
Or something that can be sold.

Thinking of this spell that those have told
Drinking like leeches off those controlled
Under the boot of a system
That was never built to question

So, if they do mention that you lack
Something we were never to contract
Consumed by a capital LIE. Spoken as fact
No, you aren't broken, It has and always was
The system that was cracked.

I'm Back

The moon and the dark
I stare, the cigarette sparks
The lights are everywhere
It's late and I'm without a care
So rare are these moments
A sweet prayer for my penance
All those close souls who I pushed away
The moon disappears

I know you are still around
Never silence, always sound
My legs hurt from the pace I move
I find the beat and feel the groove
Everyone sleeps yet I'm awake
The moon has seen every one of my mistakes

And the ash falls, while she comes back. This is the
night, when I feel, I am back on track.

Reflection

Where do I begin with you?
I whisper in my shattered refection
I know you are still in there
Somewhere. Anywhere
Seeing all these broken pieces
Stare back at me in delight
But that's a lie and why?
Do I pretend to smile?
I've missed you for awhile
As I look, I wonder all it has took
All these scars, and all these marks
Trying hard to mask, still this reflection it asks.
Who are you?
Do you know anymore?
Surely the sun will rise once more
This shattered light will end
But who are you, my only friend?
As I talk to my reflection again
Who are you? Do I know you?
Be heavenly minded. While your feet stay planted to
the ground, in all this hell that has been granted
Reflection...

A Conversation with the Devil

He welcomes me with light
The forbidden fruit, ready to bite
A cunning smile, so tempting and bright
Meet the morning star at the end of the night
They never told you of this angel's beauty
A sweet hello, to the hell I know thoroughly
Offering an alternative to my poverty
But what do I have to give?
Should I give my soul?
Promise to die young with my art will growing old?
I don't know.
He has offered this before
With so many nights of spiritual war
The price this prince of the world wants
Was not worth it in the end
For his lies lead nowhere my friend
A conversation with the devil
I'll forever remember that night
A message from a fallen angel
That can transform to light.

I Am

I feel like a lonely tree
Without compatibility
My vines spring wine
And the forest, I hardly see

One day at a time does have its appeal to me.

But I'm still drinking to cry you see
And I cry red
Yes, one day at a time does have its appeal to me

Though I am a lonely tree
Too blind to see
The forest surrounding me...

Burning Poems

It's clear, that my mind and yours
Just isn't the same anymore
As I light these pages to ash
For years this flame inside me I did try to smash
With no cash or anyone ever to hold
In the mirror is a smile, though these wrinkles are
    getting old
Told stories of delusions in my past, still though, I'm
    on fire
Desiring those past days of illusion lasted longer
    honestly
Wrong it seems to cry at a bird's peaceful song
Still I cling on
The ambers of these written words
Fly, like exactly how I wanted them too
So, I guess now, all I have are these sweet memories
    of you
But before the games
And the flames in your eyes

I was just burning poems
Reminiscing over truthful lies.

Life is a Traffic Jam

Life is a traffic jam
Roadblocks in every direction
All I see are red lights
I wish green could be seen so I could go.
But life is a traffic jam you know

Heard it in the nineties, never truer now.
Pac sore the signs,
how he did is still a mystery to me.

All these red lights and blocks seem so foul.
I ask for god's help, is he testing me now?
Life is a traffic jam you know.

This fast pace was never meant to last long.
This game stays on pause because I'm headstrong.
I see blocks and locks at every angle.
No devil, hip hop heavy metal.
But I stay still,
Life is a traffic jam with nowhere to go.
Then though.
Green...

Diary

My life certainly is a traffic jam. I was stuck and fighting against reality, it took a little while for the medication to work, so I ended up being in the hospital for a month.

And one long month it was, there were delusional people around me. Some violent, some unpredictable

One was obsessed with angels, another thought he worked for the space force, and with my mind at the time I almost believed him. It sounds funny right now, but it is also so sad how the brain can break. But just like the psychiatrist sad. It is like someone with a broken leg, or an illness. This is the purpose of my writing. I want people to understand, be aware, and hopefully comprehend with compassion not fear. It's embarrassing for me, but I am putting myself out there for others to see, this is my goal, this is my plan. Do not fear those suffering from mental illness.

I hope you understand me.

Dreamland

Being a schizophrenic, I've seen the dreamtime
I tried so hard to capture it. Express it through rhyme
Unfortunately, those around could not understand
    my mind
A delusional dreamland was the food that I was fed
It took in too much, as I indulged and drowned in
    dreams
Anything to escape. Anything to cope.
Shinning my mind's eye on those unseen realms
Jotting down my mistaken psalms.
So, if you have seen the dreamland to
Here is what I recommend that you do.
Do not be afraid to dive headfirst into the deep
But be careful that your sanity you keep.

The dreamland you see can be full of wonders
But eventually. You must wake up, or so it seems.

Fallen Fruit

Did you hear about the fallen fruit?
It learned to live low, all on its own
Surrounded by other fallen flesh
Surrounded by its mother's roots

One day though someone picked it up
Not knowing how helpful that was
When others trod past
Someone noticed it's sweetness

They saved that fallen fruit
From the dirt it lived in a long time
Without even knowing it's past
Somebody finally noticed it was sweet

And it was picked up,
At last.

Free Man

I breathe slowly
The wind touches me
It's so hard to stand still
Lost and crazy, you know the drill

I'm out of the hospital
Though never standing still
My heart though crushed
How quickly did insanity rush

So, what now and where to go?
No more bouncing to and fro
Stability is what I need
As reality plants it's little seed

I imagine I will focus on this cool breeze
Focus on my breath for ease
No longer am I caged and enraged
For I am a free man today.

Alcoholics Anonymous

Poison enters my blood stream
Queasiness fills my body
Reasoning is to many solo days
Straight to the bathroom I go
Toilets are an alcoholic's best friend
Utensils for all unwanted
Violence explodes of pain
Why did I wake up today?

Death

I heard a man once say
It's the darkness that keeps the lights on

He was dying, singing
In a shallow grave
Nowhere to be found

Now, the ground was crying
And the clouds were closing in

He was dying, singing
Covered in his sin

Yes, he was dying, singing
Waiting for death

To end, and yet to begin.

Mental State

Stained fingertips
Gold tobacco and poison sips
But whatever helps me sleep right?
Maybe I'm too blind to see proper sight
So, I top up, ready for war and another lonely night
Why fight these things done daily when you are gone
  lately

Sometimes I see demons in my smoke
Whispers in my mind, just one more toke
Then, an angel offers salvation, one clean breath of
  hope
Lord knows why we do these things to cope
But now it's getting late, time to drop all this self-
  hate.

Now you must learn to love yourself,
Wealth, it comes from a little change
I know you will rearrange your mental state
It's not at all too late,
No, It's not...

Diary

As I was dealing with my schizophrenic mind, I was still drinking nonstop to deal with the trauma that these past years have dealt me.

It's hard when everyone thinks your crazy, or simply doesn't understand what happens when someone is going through an episode. My family didn't understand my outburst, and I was scared to leave the house from fear and embarrassment of my break down, which was quite public.

At the time of course the police came, wanted to know what was wrong with me, and why I was spazzing all around the shops. "Nothing" So, they ended up leaving quickly, lucky for me.

You see you need to have some compassion for the people you see around acting weird, or those that are homeless, because you should know that they need help, not judgement.

I know what It's like to be both, which is why I now appreciate life so fully. My writing is not for the judgmental souls, but for those they put on the bottom, those who struggle in this system, that's who I am speaking for and I will put myself on the front line and be a voice for the voiceless. This is what this book is about.

This is my mission.

Mumma Said

This one is love for my Mum
A true and caring soul
Made me be true and make caring seem the only
   goal
Sure, she was stuck inside a jail of a home
Though she helped me grow.

Mumma told me to love the unwanted
And rescue those who are haunted
So, I don't do this for me but you
These words that I put out to the world
The judgement that I go through

I know I'm not special, but you made me feel that
   way.
Mumma made it clear to live for the day.
To make a better tomorrow
And No soul should live in sorrow
That's what
Mumma said.

Addiction is a Disease

Imagine waking and needing a needle
Something you know you don't want, but can't stop
It's killing you slow
You are willing to do anything for it
Step over your family if you have too

What would you do?

A junkie sits in an abandoned school
These are hard knock lessons

She is juggling sanity, has shaking hands and a
    stuttering voice
Waiting to score, but slowly losing it all.
Itching. Wishing for someone to call
Knowing the fall is coming, running from reality.
Soon there will be nowhere to run
Soon taken under
In her world no rest or ease
Now Know this
Addiction is a disease

Why We Walk
(for George Floyd)

The weary will go on
They have trod for far too long
Never resting or warm
As the corrupt continue to covert and swarm.
Though their eyes they may be tired
They will walk until their feet are red
If they must walk through gravel or over hot coal
They will. For a destination is their goal
In the journey they loudly speak
For we are the many, that are far from the peak. The
mountain remains cold and covered. Some are dead
while others recovered.
They move on despite their obstacles
One is crying while the other he chuckles
I am the foundation of this fortress
You be the hare, and I will be the tortoise
Yes, the weary continue to walk
As if this revolution is just all talk
From the bottom they holler and hoot
All over, one black man's neck and a boot

Pain

There is nothing plain about mental pain
Or emotional torture
But with these words what will they gain?

Sickness you can't see, seems so simple
But trust me, it's rough as guts
While you may put on a mask, pretending to be
    tough.

Never fear a reaching hand
And if you fall, get up again

I know the pain of the past
Though not even pain lasts

So, if you are stuck in a deep hole
Confide in that you have a soul

Sure, pain can be deep inside
But remember after all,
this is just a ride.

Loosie

The sun is shining as morning dew weeps
An old employee is watching while he sweeps.
Please look away is what the homeless man thinks.
    Bends down with a crack, as he picks the butt off
    the track

Into his pocket it goes

Half a heart for a locket on his neck.
While the other half is long buried.
He is alone now, early in the morning,
around the town he roams.

Looking for loosies...

The sun will decline once more, like his health.
No wealth and he is the butt of society,
smothered by the shadows.
The man looks down,
but there is no ease to be found.

All day looking for a smoke,
until the sun cries
and the man and the smoke,
silently goes down.

Another Rose

The weed and the misplaced flower.
One it blossoms. The other devoured
Red is the rose, and brown is the weed
The brown it wants to spread
But it chokes on those in need.

The flower it stays planted
Because its scent is already sweet
Though it still does have thorns
So, there is still some deceit

Both have an oath, to this place we call home
The flower and the weed,
And while the brown is cursed
The flower.
All alone

Darkness is just a reminder
That light exists...

Light

The Light

I hit the switch
I pace, I twitch

I dance, I sing
I only care about one thing

How are you?

I sit, and wait patient
Before I was a patient

Before I felt the needle jab
Before this book became a job

I did love you

When once every ounce of me was yours
From the dust on my feet, to the dirt in my pours

From the cracks in my mind
While yours was always a surprise what to find

But I knew you
And I thought you knew me too
Until the shade, like a blade,
cut through the glue of us two

But one question I have
How are you?

Then I notice the light of my phone
So, I answer.

A Love Story Reignited

It starts something like this
Not with a kiss, but a sweet hello
The kind of gesture that you would give a stranger.

The danger was always that I would lose myself when
    I lost you.
And like a guilty man, I did...
Thinking for a time, I could erase and get rid of that
    face from my mind's eye

Yes, I was never the white picket fence kind of guy

You quickly tell me you are in love,
and are soon to be married.
My smile must belong to a great actor.
I admit, I didn't factor another man in your plans

With that you leave, not with a kiss.
Just a bittersweet goodbye.
No need to know why you left.
But like fruit from a farmer,
we are both have now grown

I'm glad for a moment
For at a time
my heart you did own
Goodbye my love revisited
And like Bukowski once said
Good luck
And all the best...

Rainbows

After the rain
When the rainbow came
I didn't blame the storm
Because, when it did come down
The rainbow that was hidden in shame
Hidden in darkness and shame.

It took the storm
To show the beauty of the rain
That it is so easy to believe in the unseen
Especially by those, who have only seen sunshine.

The rainbow
Is beautiful but sad to me
Because those people who always live in the light
Will never get to see, all the colours it holds

This is my rainbow.

Breathe

The spirit, can you hear it?
In the wind, winding through the trees
Dancing in the breeze
Waiting for you

No, you don't need to give it praise
Or bow down to your knees
Just breathe. Breathe in that essence
If we are natural, Life should never be
A death sentence.
So, let the spirit calm your bones,
and ease your mind.
For even peace can come in time.
And the past, well we cannot rewind
Therefore, calm your mind

Breathe.
Nature really is the mother to us all
And when you silent your mind, you'll hear her call.
Now be still and meditate on this.
We are not just this fleshly body
Or this silly mind
You are way more. The universe in human form
Breathe. Yes breathe
Once more.

The Storm

In the midst of a wonderment storm
An oak tree wanted to be free
For his whole life, He was planted to the dirt
It took work through the blazing brushes
But that day, his roots were raised
He did you see, what he thought he couldn't do

He walked away
He walked from the worries of the wind
The chattering of the birds
The trauma of the storm

But what was surprising to that oak tree,
was that in the end,
it was the storm that set that him free.

Brightest Day

From my soul to yours
To get you through the storm
We all have many flaws
As we try each day to be reborn

So, when you wake from your sleep
And open up that safe
There's no need to make a peep
I won't be on your case

When you feel the light is fading
I'll remain by your side
Depression may be invading
But you know with who to confide

Look within my friend
Your heart will lead the way
It is your soul now to depend
For, from the darkest nights, comes

The brightest day.

Delusional Psalms

In my delusional psalms
I held you in my arms
And branched out like an old tree
Trying to be everything that I didn't want to be.
One crazy man out on a limb
Ready to fly just on a whim
Though unlike the birds, I crashed so hard
When my windows were covered in bars
And though these scars you could not see
They completely covered me
So now I look to the sky
And all I could think was why, why, why
But in those times, I did not die
I held the future firm in my eye
Though they were maddingly wide
I did not hide
So now it is this book
In which I confide
My notes that I jot
For days before I do rot
I have found that secret sacred spot
In which we call faith.

A Conversation with God

I remember once I asked you for a sign
And then the time came, that I heard you
Not with words, though that I could bare
Just small imprints, of proof that you were there
For years I did feel alone
And the devil he was on me
I remember pleading with you
With a storm outside, and one brewing within
Even through all my steps of sin you heard
And all you asked was listen to my word
For you've watched over me since I was born. And
stayed, even after our connection was torn
As you sat with me through my darkness
Then blessed me with your sun
When everyone beside me disappeared
You were there
Most days I didn't believe you cared
But at this divine time
There you were
Forgive me though
For I am
Just a man

Diary

Now that I have found some sort of freedom. Away from people peering at me while I would sleep, and injections that made me feel oh so low. It is time to grow.

Truth is, the hospital helped me so much, when I was sick. Inflicted with this non curable mental illness. I ended up finding once again a lust for life.

It's not that I found anything special, besides one crazy story.

Really, I do admire those people who can go about their day to day and never have to stay in a mental ward

This last time was my third visit in the ward, and my longest stay yet. Though, it is time for some light to shine I think, and with that being said, I will find a way to function as a free man. I won't just dream while I sleep.

Mona Lisa Smile

(For Lisa)

Mona Lisa smile
You work of art you

You will be great for more than awhile
With all that compassion too

Beautiful, funny and smart

So many gifts you have in your heart
Hopefully your happiness is just the start

Where do I begin?
But gin today thinking of you

It is a sin not to mention your beauty
This I feel is my duty

So, kind and so true
Why do you look so blue
I'm glad that you found love

Mona Lisa, please smile
You work of art you.

I Shall Go

Through the shimmering shallows
And salty seas. That are not dead but rising
I shall go

To many foreign lands
With nobody holding my hand
I shall go

Where the fruits grow wild
And the only illness is captivity
I shall go

On planes, and trains
That spark the membranes
Of grains
Of sand
Of stars
Of minds

Of infinite possibilities
I shall go.

Fly

I will remain strong
For sadness has been far too long

I didn't know why I wanted to die drinking
I was a caged bird hardly singing

My wings were clipped
I indulged and I sipped

This for me was unexpectable actions,
Stolen parts of my soul were taken in fractions.

I had to let go otherwise I would die
I needed to love myself

So, I could fly.

To the Fullest

To the fullest
I will drink and I will swim
I will bath in this life
On a whim trying something fresh and new
All the while loving you.

To the fullest
I will learn to forgive transgressions
I will live like I will die
Trying anything I choose
Grounded, is not my destination
So, I will fly

To the fullest
And if I fall
I will get back up
Eating this forbidden fruit
Of the knowledge of good and evil

To live.
To love.
To die

To the fullest...

So You Know

When the dark clouds dispersed
I read what you said, you thought I was cursed

As the sun silently showed some sunshine
I read one line; you said you were fine

With that I let you be.
And like that sun left the message silently

I'm glad that you are proud to call yourself a wife.
And that you finally have that white picket fence life.

It just wasn't for me
And I just wasn't for you

But we both found a little light
Now we both found a little insight
So now it's time to branch out and grow
I may have seemed mad at the time. But I am happy
for you

Just so you know...

Somehow

I am shedding my skin
Fixing the broken
While my heart still beats hard
And I remain anxiety scarred

Though while I am scared
Something inside says
Be strong.

A strange pull to do right
Has got me through the dark soul of the night

And with that I hold to hope
I will cope now
Cop it on the chin and grow
That this is my vow

I will stay in the light
Some way and
Somehow.

Souls

The souls of my shoes
Have trod through many moons
Through many hospital rooms
Worn down and worn out
A remembrance of my soul
The heat from this place,
Has melted me away
Sticking to the oily pavement
These shoes walk a path like no other
Through grassy fields and arid lands
Still, I'll never see these souls again when worn

But I continue to walk.

To God

I'm thankful I found you
And even the tests you have put me through.

I'm thankful for your guidance
And your confidence

I'm thankful that you are fair
Even when no one was there

I'm thankful for the sun, and for the moon
But most of all,

I'm thankful

That you didn't take me too soon

The Lost Sheep

The lost sheep
Who strayed from the heard
Finally found her new shepherd
When she heard his word
She was filled with disgrace
The sheep thought she could not replace
But this shepherd saw beauty
In her heart, and in her face

So, she became separated
And obligated
To lead the other lost sheep
To her shepherd
On the high hill
And while steep was the climb
The shepherd proclaimed to those lost that she found

Now, you are now mine.

My Moon
(for my mother)

I have to do another one for my mother.
The main reason is well, I love her.
She introduced me to music, and poetry.
For that I am grateful eternally.

Maybe the only women I will love
Yes, we fight, but that's alright
In my last book you said you liked the train
I hope I can replicate that again

I'm sorry I'm not as good as I want to be
Here you'll hear no great metaphors or similes

But if I were to you use some
You are like my moon
Watching over me in the dark

If I was a tree, you would be the bark
Protecting me and holding me together
So, I love you like the moon
Even if there still is darkness in me

You are my light.

Virgo Sun

I was born a Virgo sun
I used to fight for fun
Years went by and dreams were crushed
They called me crazy, so my voice I did hush.

Then I fell for an old flame
But nearly lost it all in this game
In this life, I was on the run
Wasted days, until Aquarius age came

Now all is being revealed
And my mind, it slowly healed
This is the age where the veil opens
And all I am wishing and hoping

Is that you accept me in all areas
All my love. All my fears
All my darkness. All my light
As I sit and stare at these stars tonight

Yes, I am a Virgo sun
Under this yellow one
The daylight has come
And I realise, I am not the only one

Diary

During my time in the ward, I was able to find some light. The light of a caring nurse's eyes, or the light of the stars through the hospital bars. The light of the mystics I met.

So, in the end, it wasn't all bad. Every one of us has dark times, I realise this. And while not many in the ward said good night, it was those little bits of light that got me through to the biggest and closest light of them all. Our sun.

Therefore, remember to look for the light, no matter how hard at times it seems to be to find. The sun will always rise, despite the lies, and pain. These are the things that will make you grow more than you'd ever know you could.

Somebody loves you okay. But if you think they don't. Then live and let live. And earn to love yourself.

Pills

You are my pill
You keep my mind together
Now when I look in the mirror
I now know who is staring back at me
The pitty pat of the past didn't last
Thanks to you and your chemical hug
So, now, I will take you daily
For this prescription is recommended
And I know what medicine I need
And that is

Love.

The Waiting Room

The good shepherd is waiting
I sit patient contemplating
I wonder what's wrong with her?
People gather and chat away
Here is the waiting room on a sunny day.
No needles for me
That makes me happy
I hope the patients are well
At times we all go through our own hell
Doctors should wear capes I think...
But before id escape and get lost in ink
I wait patient, with no drink
Soon the doctor I will see
Will he help me?
I hope he helps the lady next to me
She looks nervous.
I notice her scars
We all have scars, I'm coming to realize that
I lower my hat and recline
Today is not about sickness, for me at least
Yes today, I feel fine.

Reminder

Be a voice
for the voiceless
Have a heart
for the heartless
A sound mind
For those who don't
And learn to love
When others won't.

Blue Bird

Little bird fly
In this blue sky

Most of the birds don't play like they used to.
But little bird, you still do

As they continue to cut down the trees
All I'm asking you is please

Please that little bird keep flying
And keep that little bird in the blue

But still with the peace of mind that he can land.

Little blue bird fly
Stay playing free

I know you still believe in me
And little bird

I still believe in you

Whatever that Means?

To a writer
The truth is no big deal
He pours out his heart
Like he does the merlot

A lot runs through his mind
Always searching for gems
That's what he hopes to find

The writer drinks and dreams
Praying others would dream like him
He swims through imagination

Searching in the dark caves
Sometimes finding some in the sun

All in search for some truth
Not the truth, his truth

Whatever that means?

Hope

My life is water, ever flowing
The chemicals flood and now I'm knowing
One step at a time can take you miles
No frowns now, it's all smiles

I had needles pinch my skin
Therefore, the meek will always be my kin
I will bathe in everything that has been offered.
Knowing there is more to see in infrared

Though today, I only see the sun
Darkness long undone
Starring at the light that didn't blind me
For even when it was too dark to see

I had hope.

Pharmaceutical Soup

As deep as the ocean
As wide as the fields
I hold onto hope

With no boundaries of time
Where space is infinite to me
I will continue to cope

I am cleansing my mind
And clearing the rubble of the past
Call it pharmaceutical soup

Washed clean now
I've found the sound mind
That I was looking for.

Untitled 2

I have burnt enough bridges
It's time to build some
The river is overflowing
And I need timbre

I have battled enough
It is time to put my sword down
My garden needs tending
And I need peace

I have held my breath too long
It is time for some ease
The trees are giving me what I need
And I need to breathe.

Waves

The waves that I thought were drowning me,
were actually leading me to shore.
When it was too deep for me to see
I thought I couldn't take it anymore.

The wash was white and full of danger
I didn't know myself and to me I was a stranger.
With my head barely above water
And the dry land, I almost forgot her.

Though I was drowning I stayed afloat somehow.
I took a breath and made a vow
That the next time the chemicals came flooding in.
I would not dive so carelessly in

Even if I'm alone I would stay a shore
For I cannot swim in the deep anymore
Where the mystics play, I got caught in a rip
Yes, I was ripe for the taking.

So, now instead of being a slave to these waves.
It is now the waves, that I am making...

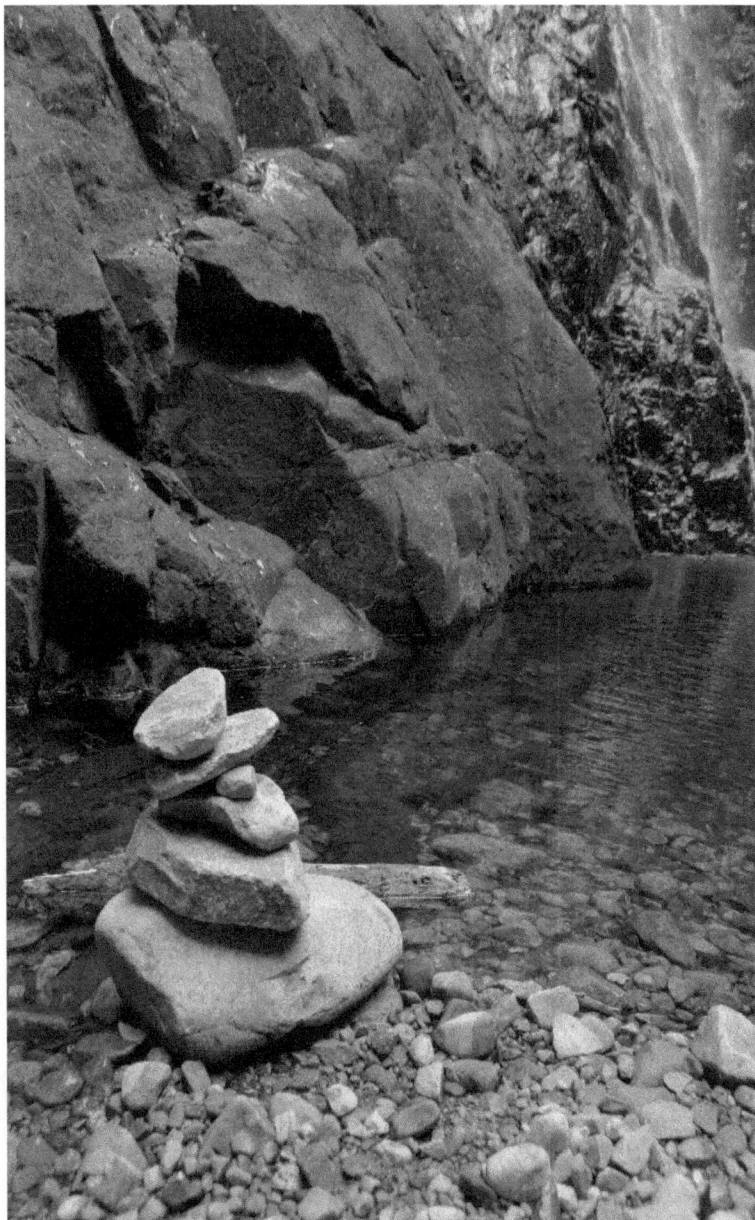

My Mast

It's time to get my life together
I have travelled through the stormy weather.
I have eaten the bad fruit before
Many times, I have hit the floor

Now I want to rise. I was never one for lies
The clouds are parting to sunny skies
I still remember your deep blue eyes

Like a comet you came into my life
One day I did hope, to make you my wife
But I couldn't contain sanities grip
And I couldn't control how much I'd sip

Now it is time though to give you my all
I do still regret our last call
But before my fall, I found this by my side
So now, before I slide

I want you to know that my love is pure
I will never forget you, or who you were
My scars. Like a storm have past
One thing will remain
You are still
my mast.

Therapy

Poetry as therapy
As I wrap another gift
Christmas came and went
Insanity came so swift

I've been writing my way through trauma
Love yourself but also your momma
But in the end, we all go out alone

At one time I fell and yelled in hospital halls.
The demons were calling me to my cage.
I came to know it so well.

This is my therapy, and I hope it does help
With that it is okay with me
Still, I found poetry, as my therapy.

Sunshine Rhymes

Waiting for the sunshine
So here I a silly little rhyme
Was I born to lose hope?
The answer
Nope...

So today I will wait for the light beams
To blast.

I am positive at last,

Let's try not to be so serious all the time

This
Is my sunshine nursery rhyme

My Poetry

Over and over, it plays in my head
The whispers under the floorboards
You should have been dead

My mind it aims for the clouds
Where a louder voice it yells out proud

This is where it begins
I saw demons as I drank from gin

I look for Allah
But I only find this empty bottle
And I try to play to the lord...

I admit I'm happy now
That I cut this chord

I'll keep this empty bottle to remind me
All I need is you now
my poetry

God's Promise
(For another Lisa)

When I was in the ward
You were with me
When I had nothing but my name
You stood by me

You fed me when I needed food
When I was surrounded by evil,
you showed me good.

You stopped my place from flooding
And did it all with your grace
Giving your love when I had no other
They always said you had a caring face

At times my delusions were wild
But you protected me from my ills

Lisa. Your name means God's promise
And now my heart has filled.

Superstitious Goodbyes

I have said goodbye before
But with a little hope I will be back again
That is what I have now
Hope.

While my brain remains grasped by this disease. I do
hope that my words offered some sort of ease.

Like the smile from a stranger
Or the feeling of no danger

Like a kid I have now let go of this balloon
And it will float wherever the wind blows
On and on it could soar, who knows?

I thought I was lost for good
That the spark of life was gone.
But I clung to my soul in that ward
And now I say that I am okay

I am sane.

Knock on wood...

Ps.
I'd like to show my greatest love if you made it to the end of my book, I truly appreciate it and hope you liked it.

Much love

Sincerely
Bradley Smith

www.ingramcontent.com/pod-product-compliance
Lightning Source LLC
Chambersburg PA
CBHW061753020426
42331CB00006B/1460

9 781960 038524